Brodie

by Iain Gray

WRITING *to* REMEMBER

79 Main Street, Newtongrange,
Midlothian EH22 4NA
Tel: 0131 344 0414
E-mail: info@lang-syne.co.uk
www.langsyneshop.co.uk

Design by Dorothy Meikle
Printed by Printwell Ltd
© Lang Syne Publishers Ltd 2023

All rights reserved. No part of this publication may be reproduced, stored or introduced into a retrieval system, or transmitted in any form or by any means (electronic, mechanical, photocopying, recording or otherwise) without the prior written permission of Lang Syne Publishers Ltd.

ISBN 978-1-85217-780-5

Brodie

MOTTO:
Unite

CREST:
A hand clutching a sheaf of arrows

TERRITORY:
Moray

NAME variations include:
- Broadie
- Broady
- Brodi
- Brody
- Broddy
- Broddie
- Brodley
- MacBrody

Chapter one:

The origins of the clan system

by Rennie McOwan

The original Scottish clans of the Highlands and the great families of the Lowlands and Borders were gatherings of families, relatives, allies and neighbours for mutual protection against rivals or invaders.

Scotland experienced invasion from the Vikings, the Romans and English armies from the south. The Norman invasion of what is now England also had an influence on land-holding in Scotland. Some of these invaders stayed on and in time became 'Scottish'.

The word clan derives from the Gaelic language term 'clann', meaning children, and it was first used many centuries ago as communities were formed around tribal lands in glens and mountain fastnesses.

The format of clans changed over the centuries, but at its best the chief and his family held the land on behalf of all, like trustees, and the ordinary clansmen and women believed they had a blood relationship with the founder of their clan.

There were two way duties and obligations. An inadequate chief could be deposed and replaced by someone of greater ability.

Clan people had an immense pride in race. Their relationship with the chief was like adult children to a father and they had a real dignity.

The concept of clanship is very old and a more feudal notion of authority gradually crept in.

Pictland, for instance, was divided into seven principalities ruled by feudal leaders who were the strongest and most charismatic leaders of their particular groups.

By the sixth century the 'British' kingdoms of Strathclyde, Lothian and Celtic Dalriada (Argyll) had emerged and Scotland, as one nation, began to take shape in the time of King Kenneth MacAlpin.

Some chiefs claimed descent from ancient kings which may not have been accurate in every case.

By the twelfth and thirteenth centuries the clans and families were more strongly brought under the central control of Scottish monarchs.

Lands were awarded and administered more and more under royal favour, yet the power of the area clan chiefs was still very great.

The long wars to ensure Scotland's

independence against the expansionist ideas of English monarchs extended the influence of some clans and reduced the lands of others.

Those who supported Scotland's greatest king, Robert the Bruce, were awarded the territories of the families who had opposed his claim to the Scottish throne.

In the Scottish Borders country – the notorious Debatable Lands – the great families built up a ferocious reputation for providing warlike men accustomed to raiding into England and occasionally fighting one another.

Chiefs had the power to dispense justice and to confiscate lands and clan warfare produced a society where martial virtues – courage, hardiness, tenacity – were greatly admired.

Gradually the relationship between the clans and the Crown became strained as Scottish monarchs became more orientated to life in the Lowlands and, on occasion, towards England.

The Highland clans spoke a different language, Gaelic, whereas the language of Lowland Scotland and the court was Scots and in more modern times, English.

Highlanders dressed differently, had different

customs, and their wild mountain land sometimes seemed almost foreign to people living in the Lowlands.

It must be emphasised that Gaelic culture was very rich and story-telling, poetry, piping, the clarsach (harp) and other music all flourished and were greatly respected.

Highland culture was different from other parts of Scotland but it was not inferior or less sophisticated.

Central Government, whether in London or Edinburgh, sometimes saw the Gaelic clans as a challenge to their authority and some sent expeditions into the Highlands and west to crush the power of the Lords of the Isles.

Nevertheless, when the eighteenth century Jacobite Risings came along the cause of the Stuarts was mainly supported by Highland clans.

The word Jacobite comes from the Latin for James – Jacobus. The Jacobites wanted to restore the exiled Stuarts to the throne of Britain.

The monarchies of Scotland and England became one in 1603 when King James VI of Scotland (1st of England) gained the English throne after Queen Elizabeth died.

The Union of Parliaments of Scotland and England, the Treaty of Union, took place in 1707.

Some Highland clans, of course, and Lowland families opposed the Jacobites and supported the incoming Hanoverians.

After the Jacobite cause finally went down at Culloden in 1746 a kind of ethnic cleansing took place. The power of the chiefs was curtailed. Tartan and the pipes were banned in law.

Many emigrated, some because they wanted to, some because they were evicted by force. In addition, many Highlanders left for the cities of the south to seek work.

Many of the clan lands became home to sheep and deer shooting estates.

But the warlike traditions of the clans and the great Lowland and Border families lived on, with their descendants fighting bravely for freedom in two world wars.

Remember the men from whence you came, says the Gaelic proverb, and to that could be added the role of many heroic women.

The spirit of the clan, of having roots, whether Highland or Lowland, means much to thousands of people.

Meanwhile, many families proudly boast the heraldic device known as a Coat of Arms,.

The central motif of the Coat of Arms would originally have been what was sometimes borne on the shield of a warrior to distinguish himself from others on the battlefield.

Clan warfare produced a society where courage and tenacity were greatly admired

Chapter two:

Ancient roots

A clan whose origins lie hidden in the dim mists of time, the Brodies feature prominently in Scotland's frequently turbulent historical record.

Not only are their roots uncertain, but also the source of the name – early versions of which include 'Brochie', ' Brode', 'Brothu', 'Brothie' and 'Brothy'.

Possible sources are from Scottish-Gaelic terms indicating 'ditch', 'mire', 'little ridge' or 'precipice', and the Irish-Gaelic 'broth', denoting 'muddy'.

But a more plausible one is the Pictish name 'Brude', 'Bruide' or 'Bridie' – with Bridie I a king of the Picts from 554 to 584.

From earliest times the Brodies were to be found in Moray – also known as The Mearns and which borders the present-day local authority areas of Aberdeenshire and Highlands – while clan tradition holds their chiefs trace a descent from the Pictish royal family of Brude.

A powerful confederation of tribes, the Picts, or Picti, were so-named by the Romans to describe 'painted or tattooed people', while other names include the Scots 'Pecht', the Welsh 'Peithwyr', the Old Norse 'Pettr' and the Old English 'Peohta'.

Flourishing from earliest times, they are thought to have been descendants of tribes including the Caledonii, while in the late ninth century their kingdom merged under Kenneth MacAlpin with the Gaelic kingdom of Dál Riata to form Alba – later better known as Scotland.

Much of the early history of the Picts has been lost to history, but mute testimony to their lives and times survives in the form of a number of intricate stone carvings.

These include the remarkable Rosemarkie Stone, or Rosemarkie Cross, named after the village in Easter Ross where its fragments were discovered under the floor of a church in the early years of the eighteenth century.

Fashioned from fine-grained sandstone, it is now proudly displayed in the village's Groam House Museum, along with other examples discovered in the area.

A 'thane' in Scots is equivalent to the rank of earl, and it was as Thanes of Brodie and Dyke, in Moray, that the early Brodie clan chiefs held sway.

Records show a Michael Brodie of Brodie receiving a charter during the reign from 1306 to 1329 of King Robert the Bruce confirming his lands of Brodie through right of succession by his paternal ancestors.

In 1466 the Brodies forged a lasting bond of kinship with Clan Mackenzie when 'John of Brode of that Ilk', 7th Chief of the Clan, helped them secure victory over their rivals Clan Donald at the battle of Blar na Pairce – the battle of the Park – near Strathpeffer, Ross and Cromarty.

But it was not only against rival clans that Clan Brodie took up the broadsword and battle-axe.

Found on the field of battle during the bitter and bloody Wars of Scottish Independence from 1296 to 1357, they also fought in other engagements with Scotland's 'auld enemy' the English.

On September 15, 1547, 'Thomame', or Thomas Brodie, the 11th chief, was killed leading his clan at the battle of Pinkie, near Musselburgh, East Lothian.

A disaster for Scotland, a 25,000-strong English army under the Duke of Somerset decisively defeated a 35,000-strong Scots force under the Earl of Arran.

Also known as the battle of Pinkie Cleugh, it was fought during the 'Rough Wooing', an attempt by England's dynastically ambitious King Henry VIII to force upon the Scots agreement for the future marriage of his son Edward to Mary Queen of Scots.

Despite their superior numbers, what led to the defeat of the Scots in what became known as 'Black Saturday', was that Somerset had the backing of a fleet of naval guns at the mouth of the River Esk.

Added to this was the early loss in the battle of the Scottish cavalry after it launched a premature and wild charge on the massed and disciplined English ranks.

Fifteen years after the battle, in 1562, Alexander Brodie of that Ilk, the 12th chief, joined

Mary Queen of Scots

with George Gordon, 4th Earl of Huntly, in his rebellion against Mary Queen of Scots.

Defeated at the battle of Corrichie, near Aberdeen, in October of that year, he was declared a rebel and his lands forfeited – but they were restored four years later after Brodie was pardoned by the queen for his previous disloyalty.

But rebellion against the Crown manifested itself again, albeit under a different monarch, during the seventeenth century Wars of the Three Kingdoms of Scotland, England and Ireland.

Also known as the British Civil Wars and of which the English Civil War formed a part, they were sparked off in Scotland during the Bishops' Wars of 1639 and 1640.

These had their origin in the widely unpopular attempt by King Charles I to impose uniform religious practice between the Church of England and the proudly independent Scottish Kirk, through the introduction into Scotland of the Episcopal Book of Common Prayer.

In turn, this acted as a catalyst for the signing on February 28, 1638 of the *National Covenant* – a document as important to Scottish history as the equally famed *Declaration of Arbroath* of 1320.

Described as 'the glorious marriage day of the kingdom with God', the Covenant renounced Roman Catholic belief, pledged to uphold the Presbyterian religion and called for free parliaments and assemblies.

First signed at Edinburgh's Greyfriars Kirk by nobles, barons, burgesses and ministers, it was subscribed to the following day by hundreds of common folk.

Copies were made and dispatched around the nation and subscribed to by thousands more – with its adherents becoming known as Covenanters.

This led to a civil war that raged between Covenanters and Royalists in Scotland from 1638 until 1649, when Charles I was beheaded on the orders of the English Parliament – whose military arm was the New Model Army under Oliver Cromwell.

One of the leading Covenanters was Alexander, Lord Brodie of Brodie, the 15th chief who, in addition to his role of 'commissioner for the apprehension of Jesuits and Catholic priests', also presided over witchcraft trials.

Commissary-General to the Army of the Covenant, he and his clan were among those who fought against the Royalist James Graham, 1st

Marquess of Montrose, at the battle of Auldearn, Nairnshire, on May 6, 1645.

The Covenanters were defeated and in the aftermath the Royalist Lord Lewis Gordon, 3rd Marquess of Huntly, sacked the Brodie scat of Brodie Castle, with many precious early records of the clan burned in the flames.

Built in 1567 on the site of an earlier castle on land believed to have been granted to the Brodies by King Malcolm IV in about 1160, Brodie Castle lies about 3.5 miles (5.5km) west of Forres, in Moray.

Originally built as a tower house, it was restored about the middle of the nineteenth century and remained the home of the Brodies until 2003 when its last resident, Ninian Brodie of Brodie, 25th Chief and also known as Brodie of Brodie, died.

His son, Alastair Ian Ninian Brodie of Brodie, the 26th Chief, died the same year and was succeeded by Alexander Tristan Duff Brodie as 27th Chief of Clan Brodie.

Now owned by the National Trust for Scotland, the castle and its magnificent grounds are open to the public and also serve as a venue for events including weddings.

Chapter three:

Fame and infamy

Bearers of the Brodie name have gained recognition through a diverse range of endeavours and pursuits.

Not only a politician but also a noted botanist, James Brodie of Brodie, 21st Chief of Clan Brodie, was born in 1744.

Educated at Elgin Academy and St Andrews University, he served as MP (Member of Parliament) for Elginshire from 1796 to 1807 and also for a time as Lord Lieutenant of Nairn.

But it was as a botanist, specialising in flora such as algae, ferns and mosses that he is best remembered.

Elected a Fellow of the Linnaean Society in 1795, his collection is now held at the Royal Botanic Garden Edinburgh, while the genus *Brodiaea* is named in his honour.

He died in 1824 while, through his marriage to Lady Margaret Duff, a sister of James Duff, 2nd Earl of Fife, he was the father of James Brodie who, while working for the East India Company, named the mansion he built in Madras 'Brodie Castle'.

He died in a boating accident in his adopted country in 1802, while Brodie Castle is now home to the College of Carnatic Music.

His paternal uncle Alexander Brodie, born in 1748, also established his fortune in India, returning to his native land a very wealthy man and buying the estates of Arnhall and The Burn, both in Kincardineshire, and Thunderton House, in Elgin.

Through his marriage to a daughter of James Wemyss of Wemyss and Lady Elizabeth Sutherland, daughter of William Sutherland, 17th Earl of Sutherland, he was the father of Elizabeth Brodie, Duchess of Gordon.

Born in 1794, the wealthy heiress married George Gordon, Marquess of Huntly and later 5th Duke of Gordon in 1813.

Described as "possessed of a handsome figure and a bright joyous disposition", she was twenty-five years younger than her husband and both had access to the glittering highest levels of society.

Despite her outward vivaciousness, however, she became distressed at the 'unblushing vice' she witnessed in such society and sought solace in intense Bible study.

Staying in Huntly Lodge, Aberdeenshire, in

the Gordon estate at Strathbogie, she embarked on what sources describe as 'a life of earnest devotion', dedicating herself to both the spiritual and educational needs of the estate tenants – particularly after the death of her husband in 1836.

Originally of the Episcopalian Christian denomination, she later became disillusioned and joined the Free Church of Scotland before her death in 1864 – the last of the Duchesses of Gordon.

Of a decidedly much different nature than the pious Elizabeth, Duchess of Gordon, William Brodie was the nineteenth century Edinburgh cabinet-maker and civic official better known to posterity as the notorious Deacon Brodie.

With 'Deacon' the title for the president of a craft trade who served on the town council Brodie, born in 1741, was highly respected and circulated among the great and the good of Edinburgh society.

But this was a facade, because for many years he had led a highly secretive life – as a burglar by night and father of five children to two separate mistresses who were unknown to one another.

Mainly to fund his amoral lifestyle Brodie utilised his expert skills as a lockwright to copy keys to cabinets he had made for wealthy clients and then to rob them.

These robberies of cash, jewellery and other valuables were carried out in collusion with partners in crime including the locksmith George Smith.

But his carefully constructed edifice of deceit suddenly crumbled following an abortive raid by Brodie and his accomplices in 1788 on an excise office in the Canongate district.

His accomplice Smith and others were arrested and Brodie, knowing his own apprehension

Deacon Brodie

was imminent, fled to London and then to Amsterdam, hoping to travel from there to a new life in America.

But he was arrested in Amsterdam and taken under heavy guard back to Edinburgh and put on trial with Smith.

Both were found guilty and hanged in October of 1788 at the Old Tolbooth, in front of an estimated crowd of 40,000.

A myth immediately grew that the gallows he was hanged from had been built by him – but it is more probable that, while he may well have been involved in its design, he did not construct it.

Myths apart, the case of Deacon Brodie gripped the popular imagination – with Robert Louis Stevenson, fascinated by the dichotomy between Brodie's public and private lives, taking him as the inspiration for his 1886 novel *The Strange Case of Dr Jekyll and Mr Hyde*.

Also in the world of fiction, the 1961 novel *The Prime of Miss Jean Brodie*, by Muriel Spark, has the titular character proudly proclaiming she is a descendant of Deacon Brodie.

A well-known hostelry in Edinburgh's Royal Mile, complete with sign bearing his image, is Deacon Brodie's Tavern, while another is located in

New York City between Eighth and Ninth Avenue and in the Canadian capital Ottawa on the corner of Elgin and Cooper.

Brodie's name is also found in Edinburgh today in the form of Brodie's Close, off the Royal Mile and where his home and workshops were located.

One bearer of the Brodie name with a rather unusual sporting claim to fame was the civil engineer John Alexander Brodie, born in Liverpool in 1858.

Having started his career in 1875 in the engineering department of the Mersey Docks and Harbour Board, he was later appointed city engineer for Liverpool.

His achievements in this role are impressive – including the Mersey Tunnel, then the world's longest underwater road tunnel, and the use of pre-fabricated housing technology to build homes more quickly and cheaply.

But a much different claim to fame came on the football pitch.

An ardent fan of Everton Football Club, he became infuriated when his team lost a match against Accrington Stanley in 1889 after having a goal controversially disallowed.

This was at a time when spectators could

stand behind the goal line and, either wittingly or unwittingly, block goals from going over.

Brodie's answer, which also aimed to solve the problem of contentious calls from match officials, was to invent the goal net.

First used during a match played at Stanley Park, in his native city, he applied for a patent and persuaded the Football Association (FA) to officially trial his invention at a game in January of 1891 between Everton and Nottingham Forest at the latter club's Town Ground in what was then the North versus South fixture.

Not only did the goal net prove a resounding success, but an added bonus for Brodie was that his beloved team won 3-0 – with the first goal scored by Fred Geary making him officially recognised today as the first footballer ever to "hit the back of the net".

Following Brodie's death in 1934 – the same year in which work on the Mersey Tunnel was completed – Liverpool Town Council named Brodie Avenue in his honour, while an English Heritage Blue Plaque commemorates the home where he lived for many years on Ullet Road.

Chapter four:

On the world stage

A pioneering American computer programme and software inventor, Richard Brodie was born in 1959 in Newton, Massachusetts.

Having studied applied mathematics and computer science at Harvard College, he joined Xerox Corporation's Advanced Systems Division (ASD), in Palo Alto, California in 1977, aged only 18, working with Charles Simonyi in the development of the Bravo X word processor for the Alto computer.

Moving with Simonyi to Microsoft in 1981 and becoming a founding member of its Application Division, he created the first version of the indispensable writing tool Microsoft Word – in less than seven months.

Also creating the original version of Notepad, he was appointed technical assistant to Microsoft founder Bill Gates in 1983, overseeing the programme that became Word for Windows.

Leaving the company for a time but returning in 1991 as chief software designer, he was the lead developer of the Omega project that was released a year later as Microsoft Access.

In addition to his interests in the world of computing, Brodie has also explored a number of 'personal self-improvement quests', resulting in books including his 1993 *Getting Past OK: The Self-Help Book for People Who Don't Need Help* and the 1995 *Virus of the Mind*.

With the fruits of her work hailed as among the most important contributions to cancer cure, **Angela Hartley Brodie** was the British biochemist born in 1934 in Oldham, Lancashire, a daughter of the industrial chemist Herbert Hartley.

After studying chemical pathology, she worked for a number of years in Shrewsbury, Massachusetts, where she met her husband and fellow biochemist Harry Brodie.

Working with him on the development of oral contraceptives, she later focussed on the study of breast cancer, finding an inhibitor to combat the enzyme known as aromatase.

This led to the development of formestane, the first aromatase inhibitor that, after a number of clinical trials, was finally marketed in 1994.

Appointed a Fellow of the American

Association for Cancer Research in 2013, she died four years later.

A pioneer of research into bone and joint disease, **Sir Benjamin Collins Brodie**, 1st Baronet, was the English physiologist and surgeon born in 1783 in Winterslow, Wiltshire.

Studying medicine at Charterhouse School, London and St George's Hospital, where he subsequently worked as a surgeon for more than thirty years, his ground-breaking work was the 1818 treatise *Pathological and Surgical Observations on the Diseases of the Joints*.

This led to a new approach by surgeons in the treatment of diseases of the joints that resulted in a significant reduction in the number of amputations and the saving of many lives.

A physician to members of the royal family including Queen Victoria and made a baronet in 1834, he was also the recipient of a number of other honours that include fellowship of the Royal Society – while Henry Gray dedicated his famous *Gray's Anatomy*, first published in 1858, to Brodie.

First president of the General Medical Council (GMC), he died in 1862, while his son **Sir Benjamin Collins Brodie**, 2nd Baronet, was the leading chemist who pioneered work on peroxides. Born in 1817 and a recipient of the Royal Society's Royal Medal, he died in 1880.

Recognised as the founder of modern pharmacology, **Bernard Brodie** was the chemist and researcher on drug therapy born in England in 1907.

Immigrating at an early age with his family to the United States and receiving a doctorate in chemistry from New York University in 1935, he went on to develop along with Julius Axelrod the therapeutic drug paracetamol.

Also pioneering a drug therapy for gout, the use of procainamide for severe irregularities in heart rhythm, studying the use of anti-psychotic drugs and a member of the National Academy of Sciences, he died in 1989.

From medicine to the world's oceans, James William Brodie, better known as **Jim Brodie**, was the geologist and oceanographer born in 1920 in Babington, Cheshire.

Immigrating with his family to New Zealand and having studied geology at Victoria University College, in 1954 he became a founding member of the Oceanographic Institute and led it from 1958 to 1977.

A Fellow of the Royal Society of New Zealand and the recipient of an OBE for services to oceanography, he died in 2009.

One inventive bearer of the Brodie name who was instrumental in saving thousands of soldiers from injury and death on the battlefield, **John Leopold Brodie** was the entrepreneur born Leopold Janno Braude in 1873 in Riga, Latvia.

Having settled in London after accruing a fortune from the South African gold and diamond mines, his attention turned during the First World War to the design of a new steel combat helmet after hearing the War Office Invention Department had rejected a French design as not strong enough.

The result was Brodie's Steel Helmet, or The Brodie Helmet, constructed from a single thick sheet of steel with a shallow, circular crown with a wide brim around the edge, leather liner and leather chinstrap.

Originally designed to protect the wearer's head and shoulders from shrapnel bursts above the trenches, the first million had been produced by the summer of 1916.

Adopted by the U.S. Army as the M1917 Helmet and colloquially known by British troops as the 'Tommy helmet', 'tin hat' and, for officers, the 'battle bowler', by the end of the war more than 7.5 million Brodie Helmets and 1.5 million M1917s had been produced.

Having seen a number of modifications to his original design, Brodie died in 1945.

From the battlefield to the stage, **Don L. Brodie** was the American actor, dialogue coach and director born in 1904 in Cincinnati, Ohio.

With film credits that include the 1935 *Manhattan Moon*, the 1945 film noir *Detour* and the 1989 *Goodnight, Sweet Marilyn* and also noted for his voiceover work on the Disney cartoon features *Dumbo* and *Pinocchio*, he died in 2001.

From the stage to sport, **Michael Brodie**, born in Manchester in 1974, is the British former professional boxer whose wins include the 2002 World Boxing Foundation (WBF) title and, a year later, the International Boxing Organisation (IBO) featherweight title.

From sport to music, **Paul Brodie** was the internationally-renowned Canadian saxophonist born in 1934.

His playing features on the soundtrack of the 1978 Academy Award-winning film *Heaven Can*

Wait, while he also wrote the tutorial *A Student's Guide to the Saxophone*.

Made an Officer of the Order of Canada in 1994 for "having shown true mastery of his art through his ability to reach all ages with his music", he died in 2007.

A Scottish sculptor whose legacy survives to this day in the form of the world-famous Greyfriars Bobby Fountain in Edinburgh, **William Brodie** was born in 1815, the son of a Banff shipmaster.

Moving to Aberdeen as a child and later apprenticed as a plumber, he spent his spare time at the city's Mechanic's Institute, casting lead figures of celebrities of the day and small medallion portraits.

Encouraged by the eminent Scottish historian John Hill Burton, he moved to Edinburgh to study at the Trustee's School of Design, followed by study in Rome.

He exhibited at the Great Exhibition of 1851 in Hyde Park, London, with characters from Charles Dickens' *Old Curiosity Shop*, but his most famous work is the Greyfriars Bobby Fountain.

Fashioned from granite, it is surmounted by a bronze life-size statue of the Skye terrier, Bobby, reputed to have spent fourteen years guarding the grave in Greyfriars Kirkyard of his owner John Gray, before dying on January 14, 1872.

Commissioned by Lady Burdett-Coutts, president of the ladies committee of the Royal Society for the Prevention of Cruelty to Animals (RSPCA), shortly before Bobby died and with the bronze statue made from life and sited near the kirkyard, it was unveiled on November 15, 1873.

Brodie, an associate of the Royal Scottish Academy (RSA), died in 1881, while his memorial to the faithful dog has the unusual honour of being Edinburgh's smallest listed structure.

One particularly daredevil bearer of the Brodie name was **Steve Brodie**, who achieved fame after claiming to have survived a jump from New York's Brooklyn Bridge.

Doubts persist to this day over the veracity of his claim, but it was largely accepted at the time that on July 23, 1886, the 25-year-old jumped from a height of 135ft (41m) – the equivalent of the height of a fourteen-storey building – from the East River Bridge, as it was known up until 1915.

Just over a year earlier, Robert Odlum Emmet, a swimming instructor from Washington, D.C., had been killed attempting the feat and Brodie is said to have practised for his attempt by making shorter jumps from other bridges and from ships' masts.

Two newspaper reporters claimed to have witnessed the event and no less an authority than the *New York Times* backed Brodie's account.

Sceptics, however, claimed that the then unemployed Brodie, in order to win a $200 bet, staged the incident along with others by a dummy being thrown from the bridge and Brodie surreptitiously entering the river from a rowing boat.

In his 1972 book *The Great Bridge*, the historian David McCullough also claims a dummy was thrown from the bridge and that Brodie had swam from shore and surfaced beside a passing barge.

But, whatever the truth, Brodie became an instant celebrity.

Taking to the stage, he appeared in the vaudeville musicals *On the Bowery* and *Mad Money* and opened a saloon in the Bowery district of Manhattan.

Portrayed by George Raft in the 1933 film *The Bowery*, he died in 1901, while his legacy survives in the form of the American vernacular expression 'to do a Brodie', meaning to take a leap, or chance – particularly a suicidal one.